February 2024

ZANE GREY EXPLORER

THE JOURNAL OF ZANE GREY'S WEST SOCIETY

Zane Grey

in Newfoundland

Zane Grey's West Society

Is organized as a charitable, not-for-profit membership association. Its purpose is to promote interest in and knowledge of the eminent American author Zane Grey and his works; to revive interest in the writings of Zane Grey; to identify, memorialize, encourage and assist in the preservation of the sites of his writings; and to encourage modern readers to read and study his life and works so that future generations may realize Zane Grey's contributions to the development of Western and outdoor adventure stories in American literature.

CALENDAR OF EVENTS

April 27, 2024
    Zane Grey Family Day at the National Road / ZG Museum (Norwich, OH)

July 13, 2024
    Zane Grey Festival at the Zane Grey Museum (Lackawaxen, PA)

October 10-13, 2024
    Pre-Convention activity (The Lone Pine Film Festival; Lone Pine, CA)

October 14-17, 2024
    42nd Annual ZGWS Convention (Lone Pine, CA)

October 18-19, 2024
    Post-Convention Trip (Death Valley / Mount Whitney, CA)

ZGWS Social Media Initiatives

Our Website: https://www.zgws.org

Our Archives: https://www.zgws.org/archives

Our Facebook page: https://www.facebook.com/ZaneGreysWestSociety

Our Instagram page: https://www.instagram.com/zanegreysws

Our Twitter page: https://twitter.com/zanegreysws

Our YouTube channel: https://www.youtube.com/channel/UCanMWlcZJCpthQqBgWlzAeg

ZANE GREY EXPLORER

Published quarterly by
ZANE GREY'S WEST SOCIETY
Contact ZGWS at:
3417 Streamside Circle # 405
Pleasanton, CA 94588-4181

OFFICERS
President
Rosanne Vrugtman, PhD.
xun@sbcglobal.net — 239-913-9242

Vice President
Dr. Alan Pratt
a.pratt53@att.net

Secretary / Treasurer
Sheryle Hodapp
sheryle@zgws.org — 925-699-0698

Immediate Past President
Terry Bolinger
tbolinger@zgws.org

Executive Director
Dr. Joe L. Wheeler
mountainauthor@gmail.com

Facebook Coordinator
Ed Meyer
ed@kekanab.com — 435-819-0201

DIRECTORS
Kristie Adney
Harvey Leake
John Sanders
Dan Terrick

***Explorer* Co-Editors**
Robert Lentz and Barbara Lentz

Distribution Editor
Terry Bolinger

Proofreader
Kathleen Raffoul

Publication Address
c/o Robert and Barbara Lentz
106 Quaker Avenue
Randolph, NJ 07869
E-mail: b2lentz@outlook.com
Phone: 973-537-5956

CONTENTS FOR VOLUME 9 ISSUE 1

CO-FOUNDERS OF ZANE GREY'S WEST SOCIETY

Dr. Joe L. Wheeler. Born in St. Helena, Napa Valley, in 1936. Both parents fifth-generation Californians. Home-schooled by a remarkable teacher / elocutionist mother. Half of childhood spent in Latin America, where parents were missionaries. Returned to U.S. in 1952. Academic work: Pacific Union College, B.A. in History (1959); M.A. in Teaching of History (1963); M.A.in English; Sacramento State University (1968); Ph.D. in English (History of Ideas); Vanderbilt University (1975); doctoral dissertation on Zane Grey. Edited and published *Zane Grey's West* with Associate Editor G. M. Farley (1979-91). Co-founded Zane Grey's West Society with G. M. Farley (1983). Continues to serve as its Executive Director. Author and editor of numerous books and collections. Considered one of America's leading anthologizers of stories. Dr. James Dobson (*Focus on the Family*) dubbed him "America's Keeper of the Story."

G. M. Farley, (1927-1992). Reared in a religious family in Kayford, West Virginia. Enlisted in Navy (1945). Served in South Pacific. Returned to West Virginia. Worked in coal mines; became a missionary. Director of Worldwide Evangelistic Missionary Outreach; Regional Director of Pentecostal Church; Pastor of Trinity Bible Church in Hagerstown, Maryland. He never forgot the Zane Grey stories his mother read aloud to him, and reached out to other Grey fans. Author of numerous books. Published the first Zane Grey fanzine, *The Zane Grey Collector* (1968). Co-founded Zane Grey's West Society with Dr. Joe Wheeler (1983). First recipient of the Society's coveted Purple Sage Award.

FRONT COVER

Newfoundland artist Clayton Hann provides this watercolor of Zane Grey enjoying his favorite activity. Read about the search for Zane Grey's Newfoundland connections in Ed Meyer's article on page 18. Photo courtesy of Clayton Hann.

Meanwhile, Back at the Ranch . . .
(Issue One, 2024)

by Rosanne Vrugtman, PhD.

One and one is two, two and two is four, and five'll get you ten if you know how to work it.

–Mae West, *My Little Chickadee* (1940, Universal)

Can't remember the last time I found myself quoting Mae West but this is one of my favorite funny lines from the classic Western movies I love so much. This curious bit of advice from Mae—as the unlikely schoolmarm in *My Little Chickadee,* alongside the bumbling but incomparable W. C. Fields—always makes me laugh. Sometimes it even has implications for everyday life.

A Western farce, *Chickadee* is not a Zane Grey film, of course, so we won't be screening that one at our 2024 Lone Pine (CA) convention. However, I hope you'll all join us for what I confidently predict will be another unique and special convention. Theme: "The Films of Zane Grey." I recommend making a note of these dates:

Pre-Convention: — The Lone Pine Film Festival

Thursday-Sunday, October 10-13 (Columbus Day weekend). This annual event is not Society-sponsored, but some may wish to attend the festivities prior to our own convention.

Convention: Monday-Thursday, October 14-17

Location: Historic Dow Villa Hotel

Many Grey movies were filmed in the nearby Alabama Hills, notably: *Riders of the Purple Sage* (the 1925 Tom Mix version), *Sunset Pass, Nevada* and *Code of the West* (the silent versions). We are currently deciding which ZG films to show at the convention, possibly at the Lone Pine Theater, if we can arrange it.

This year's convention book will be *Wanderer of the Wasteland*, which should be of special interest, since the Post-Convention trip is a venture into the area described in the book. More info soon about main convention plans, including amenities and attractions.

The 1925 Riders of the Purple Sage.
*The movie was lensed in the Alabama Hills region near Lone Pine, where we will be visiting during our 2024 annual convention.
Photo courtesy of ZGWS.*

Post-Convention: Death Valley / Mt. Whitney

Friday-Saturday, October 18-19

These two locations, respectively, are the lowest and highest points in the lower forty-eight states. Wouldn't it be fascinating to be able to say you visited both extremes in a single tour on a single day! We sent a blast notification about the post-convention trip last week because this popular venue fills early. We recommend reserving your lodging quickly if interested.

Mt. Whitney Web Cam image
Source: http://www.whitneyzone.com/

In other news,

Zoom Board Call—January 17

Periodically during the year, the ZGWS board members meet via Zoom call to discuss needs and plans. Our first Zoom call this year was held on January 17th. Our agenda and presenters:

The annual convention (Todd Newport)

Todd is spear-heading planning for the 2024 convention. Our itinerary for the convention is still very tentative, while we discuss details like presenters, presentations, movies, tours and possible event activities. We'll provide more specific info as details are finalized. Meantime, you can review some of the proposed details at: https://www.zgws.org/zgws_annual_convention.php.

President's note: We had great fun with the lively "pop-up" activity last year—"My Favorite ZG Book and Why." I'm proposing as this year's pop-up topic: "My Favorite ZG Character and Why." Start thinking now. Be ready!

Membership Renewals (Sheryle Hodapp)

2024 member renewals are underway. While we wait for some of our January expirations to renew, Sheryle reported on the current status: 177 paid memberships, with a January expiration pool of 109 members. We've had 63 January 24 renewals to date (26 digital only/37 print plus digital); renewal pending for 46 members. Another 62 memberships will expire sometime between February and December 2024.

President's note: If you are one of the 46 pending January renewals, we hope you'll get in touch soon. This will help us to calculate our likely income for 2024 and budget accordingly. It will also ensure that you don't miss any upcoming issues of the Explorer.

Explorer (Terry Bolinger)

Terry reports that *Explorer* plans are progressing well. We'll be sending a link for the digital version to everyone, since "Print Plus" memberships will include access to the digital version of the journal, as well.

President's note: Elsewhere in this issue, you'll find Terry's article about accessing the digital Explorer. We'll be testing the procedures with this issue and refining as we go along. Feel free to send along your feedback and/or suggestions.

Membership Benefits (Terry Bolinger)

Terry also proposed a number of ideas for expanding member benefits. For instance:

We could provide a bonus download with each digital issue of the *Explorer*. This could be one of the forty-two Grey works currently in the public domain, in PDF format, along with bonus content similar to that included with the *Centennial Edition* works—articles on geography, movies, essays, etc.

We could provide some of the early non-fiction magazine articles (e.g., "The Man Who Influenced Me the Most"). Each digital document would become part of the ZGWS Digital Library, as well.

We could offer a quarterly Zoom session—book or trip discussion, collecting seminar, etc. These would be much like those we produced in lieu of the 2020 convention.

We could also conduct an online fund-raising auction each year.

President's note: I love all of these ideas! The one catch, as with every great idea we devise, is finding one or more volunteers to ramrod the process or assist the ramrod. Interested? Please get in touch with Terry or me.

Endowment (Sheryle Hodapp)

Sheryle, who watches our Endowment Fund closely, reported on its current status. To show how the fund see-saws, balances (in 10s of 1000s) for the last several months were: August: $209K. September: $206K. October: $207K. November: $215K. December: $224K. Mid-January: $229K (our highest total to date). Two days later, the fund was down to $226K. Despite market volatility, we have continued to enjoy good growth. In fact, with recent donations and fund growth, we anticipate having our first funds available for use sometime this year.

President's note: The Endowment Committee, headed by Alan Pratt, is busy producing Endowment funding guidelines. It is likely that our first monies will be invested in a redesign of the Society website. Terry is already working on finding a designer so we can get an estimated cost to consider. We will keep members posted as plans progress.

Budget (Alan Pratt)

Facilitated by Alan, the group held a general discussion about likely expenses moving forward. We're in a bit of a flux about funding for 2024 while we await the balance of our renewals. At present, however, we believe 2024 levels will closely compare with those from 2023, and we anticipate having adequate funding to cover our needs this year. We are also looking for alternate revenue streams.

President's note: Naturally, we'll keep a close eye on income and expenses and update members on budget matters as we go along.

My final thoughts —

Thanks to all of our board and members for continued input and support. Special thanks to Todd as our 2024 convention coordinator, along with Sheryle, Terry, and all who are helping with this duty. Those who haven't done this job may have no idea how much time and effort are needed to put together a well-organized, apparently seamless convention each year. Please be sure to add your thanks to mine when you see these folks in Lone Pine.

Additional thanks to Dan Terrick, who has offered to gather location and cost information for a 2025 convention in Wheeling, West Virginia—to be presented at the 2024 business meeting for your consideration. If anyone is willing to do some coordination and put together a presentation on another location, please let me know. We'd love to have *two* 2025 convention locations to present for your consideration. Meanwhile, we are preparing for this year's event. We hope to see ALL of you at Lone Pine in October. Conventions are not the same without you there!

Many surprises still to come. Please begin making your plans now!

Finally, in the fifteen years since I joined ZGWS the Society has become family to me. I want to acknowledge the recent loss of my dear friend Eleanor, who adopted me as an honorary third daughter along with "sisters" Pam and Dolli. Eleanor survived COVID at 99, celebrated her 100th birthday party via Zoom, and lived to see 103. Dear "Mom," you are sorely missed. Happy trails to you and all those we've lost over the years. See you at the round-up.

More anon,

Rosanne

Eleanor at Mormon Lake, 2009.

ZGWS 42nd Annual Convention - Lone Pine, CA

October 14th through October 17th, 2024

by Todd Newport

Our annual ZGWS Convention will be taking place in one of the most famous western movie locations in the world, Lone Pine, California. The convention will immediately follow the Lone Pine Film Festival (LPFF), which will provide our members the opportunity to arrive early and experience an event that's been held since 1990 in Lone Pine. The LPFF will occur from October 10 through the 13th, and our ZGWS Convention will begin on Monday, October 14.

Our plans for the ZGWS Convention are still forming but we have already reserved our hotel, the Historic Dow Villa, which is now one hundred years old and full of great western history. So make sure to get your reservations in for Monday through Thursday (10/14—10/17) that week (see the hotel instructions, provided separately). This location is just minutes from the famous Alabama Hills that sit between Lone Pine and the eastern side of the Sierras which tower above Lone Pine just to the west. There were a dozen Zane Grey movies filmed in and around Lone Pine and Death Valley just to the east.

We are trying to finalize a location for our first event, the opening BBQ on Monday night, right in the Hills if we can pull it off. What a great way to start our week!

On Tuesday we will have a few speakers as usual, and these are looking to be quite interesting and informative. That day we will also hold our annual auction to raise money for the Society, so get ready to do your part and bid often. Of course, we are always looking for really cool material to make available, so be thinking about what you might donate. We are also planning to have our much-anticipated Ice Cream Social, members book sale and book signings if we have authors attending.

Wednesday we are planning a trip to the Alabama Hills to locate several ZG movie locations for some "then and now" photos. We may also be able to locate a few other non-ZG movie locations as there are so many out in "the rocks." We should also have time for another presentation, dinner on one's own, and then an evening movie presentation from a movie expert (hopefully Dr. Jim D'Arc!) featuring one of the movies filmed in that region.

Thursday will have us conducting our business meeting and holding another presentation followed by lunch on one's own and then our annual book discussion. The book this year will be *Wanderer of the Wasteland*, the title that brought ZG to Death Valley to do more research to be able to complete the novel he believed would be his finest. *Wanderer of the Wasteland* was filmed three times, in 1924, 1935, and 1945, with the first being filmed in Death Valley and the next two lensed in Lone Pine. Thursday will also be the final day of our convention and we will hold the closing banquet to complete the week.

For our Post-Convention Trip we will travel about two hours into Death Valley National Park to spend Friday and Saturday exploring the area and possibly matching some old Zane Grey photos to their actual locations. See the map for details. We will be staying at the Ranch at Death Valley for Friday night. There is a very interesting restaurant there where we will try to get the group together called "The Last Kind Words Saloon."

There are several places to eat in Lone Pine and you will be able to pick from many different types (Asian, pizza, BBQ, traditional etc.) of food each day; we do not have a group meal. While in the Lone Pine area you will want to visit several locations of interest. We will try to get the group into the Lone Pine Film History Museum together as it is a must see while in Lone Pine. Below is a list of places that you may want to visit (you can find their websites online):

Lone Pine Film Festival

For those of you that would like to attend this great event prior to the ZGWS Convention

Museum of Western Film History – Located in Lone Pine, CA (in town)

Mount Whitney

The highest peak in North America outside of Alaska and 25 minutes from Lone Pine

Manzanar National Historic Site (U.S. National Park Service) (nps.gov)

This a very interesting location with a great museum and exhibits, about 15 minutes

Alabama Hills / Bureau of Land Management (blm.gov)

History of Dow Villa – Dow Villa Motel

The history of our hotel in Lone Pine

The Ranch At Death Valley / The Oasis at Death Valley

Death Valley National Park (U.S. National Park Service) (nps.gov)

If you have any questions about our ZGWS convention or the Lone Pine Film Festival feel free to contact Todd Newport (email at tbnewport@cox.net or text/call at 928-273-0299). Todd is leading the planning committee for this event,

2024 Post-Convention Trip Plans

by Rosanne Vrugtman, PhD.

This year's convention will be held in Lone Pine, CA, the site where multiple Zane Grey movies (and many, many others) were filmed. Look for more details on the convention hotel and convention registration soon, but we want to mention some Post-Convention Trip plans, as you might want to start making arrangements for this, if you are interested in joining us.

The event will be held at Death Valley National Park, about a two hour drive from Lone Pine on the way to Las Vegas (Nevada!). There are several lodging options in the Park and most event attendees are planning on staying at the Furnace Creek location. There are two lodging options at Furnace Creek – the Ranch and the Oasis. The Ranch has several room options and has the least expensive lodging (other than a campground) at Furnace Creek. The Oasis is more expensive. Death Valley National Park lodging is very popular and the lodging will be filling quickly. So, if you're interested in the post-convention trip, we encourage you to make your reservations earlier rather than later.

This event is just a "come on your own" activity. While there will be several ZGWS members staying at the park, there will be no formal activities or events planned but maybe we'll be able to meet up and take some group photos. Attendees can pick and choose what they want to do in the park – whether it's just sightseeing or something more adventurous such as hiking.

The actual convention will be held Monday, October 14th – Thursday October 17th, in Lone Pine, CA, and the plan is to get up Friday morning, October 18th, check out of the convention hotel and then drive over to Death Valley National Park and eventually end up at Furnace Creek, which is less than a two hour drive (105 miles).

Several attendees are planning on staying at Furnace Creek for the nights of Friday, October 18th and Saturday, October 19th. If you would like to join us, here is the online link for the Furnace Creek lodging in Death Valley National Park:

https://www.nps.gov/deva/planyourvisit/lodging.htm

Select either The Inn at Death Valley (under The Oasis at Death Valley) or the Ranch at Death Valley (under the second The Oasis at Death Valley). One comment – when you make reservations, they will go ahead and charge you for one night.

Furnace Creek also has a campground, if you would like to camp. The weather at Death Valley this time of year is a bit unpredictable but it shouldn't be as terribly hot as it would be in September. There is also lodging in a couple of other places in the park, including Stovepipe Wells. But Furnace Creek is the most popular lodging area.

Grey visited Death Valley in early 1920, in preparation for writing *Wanderer of the Wasteland* (our convention book) and in fact, walked across the valley floor from Furnace Creek. We have vintage photos of Grey in Death Valley and we know the location of several of these photos (some are very easy to reach – right on the road) and can share those with you, if you're interested.

If you are planning on attending the convention and have never been to Death Valley, we really want to encourage you to take advantage of this opportunity and spend some time at Death Valley. It's an amazing place with lots to see and do.

If you plan on joining us for this event and make reservations, please let us know so that we can know how many to expect.

The Wonderful World of Digital (*Explorer*s, That Is)

by Terry Bolinger

As most of you know, the Board of Directors and officers of Zane Grey's West Society have determined that after thirty years, our membership dues need to be increased in order to support the funding of the Society's administrative functions. I won't go into that in any more detail, as it's been discussed in other places. A necessary consequence is that we must move to a more digital focused membership, specifically dealing with the digital *Explorer* – our journal provided in a PDF format. This is going to be a long article so I will provide you with an outline of what I'll be discussing.

- How will the digital *Explorer* be distributed?

- How do I read a digital *Explorer*?

- Instructions for reading a digital *Explorer* on an Amazon Kindle / Kindle app

- Instructions for reading a digital *Explorer* on a Barnes & Noble Nook / Nook app

- How to find FREE Zane Grey eBooks

- How to make your own Zane Grey eBooks

- Additional content the Society can (and should) make available digitally

Moving to digital distribution is the wave of the future. Many other societies, organizations and groups have already moved away from print distribution to digital distribution. I receive newsletters from a historical society – I used to get print copies (4– 6 copied pages) in the mail. Now I get emails from them with documents attached. In our case, we understand that many members want to read print copies, rather than digital copies. That's why we are offering both options, believing that it is the best compromise considering all options. But we understand that the initial move to digital reading can be challenging for some.

Also, recognize that those of you who opt for printed copies (at the higher cost membership level) will also receive digital copies (assuming that you have provided us with your email address). The two membership classes are called Digital and Print Plus (Digital).

How will the digital *Explorer* be distributed?

The ZGWS officers and directors understand that the *Explorer* is one of the primary benefits of the ZGWS. Therefore, we want to protect it and limit distribution to members only, as much as possible. The ZGWS has several different methods where the digital *Explorer* could be accessed, such as our website and / or our digital archives. However, the easiest method is going to be use a Society Dropbox account and provide a shared link. This link will come in an email to all members with an email address – merely click on the link and it will bring up the document in your PDF reader application on your PC or your mobile device. You can then choose to save it to a location of your choice or even print it.

Anyone with this link will be able to download the document so we are counting on our members to not share the link with anyone outside of the Society. If we see many more downloads than expected, we will address the issue, but we're not expecting this to happen.

Our plan is to protect the last two years' worth of *Explorer*s for members. Remember that our stated goal is to educate the public about Zane Grey and our journals are one of the best ways to do that, but at the same time, we want newer information to go to our members first. We're walking a fine line on this so after two years, we will add older journals to our website, allowing the public to view them if so desired.

How do I read a digital *Explorer*?

Ok, now we're reaching the crux of the matter. As I talk to people about digital vs. paper, I hear the comment over and over again that "I want to have the paper in my hand and I don't want to read the Explorer on my computer." I get it.

I used to be in this camp with respect to reading paper books vs. eBooks. I wanted to read paper. Then, several years ago, my wife Bobbie received a Barnes & Noble Nook eReader as a gift. She began buying eBooks vs. print books (eBooks were almost always cheaper than the print copy) and she loved it. She practically never reads a print book anymore. I took the plunge and read an eBook (a ZG eBook of course!) and it changed my mind – now I prefer to read eBooks over print. There are several reasons for that.

First, I can read an eBook with one hand. I don't have to worry about having the book's pages flip over on me as it lays open. I can be eating or drinking something and effortlessly be reading the eBook concurrently. A simple swipe on the screen with one finger changes the page. Second, I can have my whole library on an eBook reader and it takes up practically no space. And it's easy to take with me on a plane or while traveling. Third, I can read an eBook in the dark – the pages are illuminated but the effect is not so annoying that it bothers others (including late at night on an airplane).

But I digress. You didn't want to know why I use an eBook – I want to describe various methods on how to read a digital copy of the *Explorer*. Even though you can read the *Explorer* on your personal computer, that is not the only way to read it digitally. You can also use an eReader device or a mobile device, such as an iPad or your mobile phone.

The obvious way – read the digital *Explorer* on your PC

This is the no-brainer way – open the *Explorer* email on your PC, click on the link in the email, and it opens on your screen. It's easy to read and easy to save to your preferred storage location. But, many of you may not wish to read the *Explorer* on your PC.

Read the digital *Explorer* on your smartphone

This is going to be one of the more common ways to read the digital *Explorer*. Most of you have a smartphone – more than likely an Android device or an Apple iPhone. This is super easy. You probably receive email on your smartphone already – when the email from the ZGWS comes with the link to the *Explorer*, open the email, then merely click on the link. Your default PDF reader will open (you might have to choose an option) and the document will open for you. Quick and easy! You're ready to read. Then, you will also have a means to save the document to your cloud or device storage.

There is one downside to this quick and easy option. The *Explorer* will open full size on the screen but the image will be so small as to make it very difficult to read. You can easily "reverse pinch" the document and make it much larger, but then it will not fit on the small phone screen. So, you'll have to swipe sideways and up and down to read the full text. But, it's extremely simple to access the *Explorer*.

Read the digital Explorer on your Tablet device

I don't own a dedicated eReader device such as an Amazon Kindle or a Barnes & Noble Nook. Instead, I own and use an Apple iPad mini (I used it for work). Using the tablet to read the digital *Explorer* is identical to using a smartphone – just click on the link in the email and it will open the *Explorer* for reading.

However, as compared to a smartphone, typically the screen of your tablet is large enough to allow easy reading of the *Explorer* without having to resort to "pinching" and swiping. Plus, color images in the *Explorer* look great on the tablet's screen!

Both Kindle and Nook have applications that can be downloaded onto the device (smartphone and tablet) and can turn your tablet into an eBook reader. That's how I read ebooks. The iPad does much more than a dedicated eReader like the Kindle or Nook. Granted, the iPad is more expensive than a dedicated eReader but it does a lot more.

I can browse the web, read email, watch YouTube videos (there are some great old Zane Grey movies on YouTube to watch as well as our ZGWS YouTube channel), and much more, all while sitting in front of the TV (sort of) watching a football game.

And you can import the digital *Explorer* into your Kindle, other eReader, or to an app very easily. Once you import it, it's just like reading any other eBook.

Another advantage of eBooks – if the document you want to read includes images, those images will normally be much more impressive on an iPad or smartphone.

Instructions for reading the digital *Explorer* on your Kindle or in the Kindle app.

First, let me say that if you don't own a Kindle, Nook, or other eReader and you're going to use an app on your PC and mobile device or you're going to buy an eReader – my personal opinion — go with either an actual Kindle device or use the Kindle app on a tablet like the iPad or your smartphone. It is much easier and more full featured than the Nook device and app. But, one comment – in order to use a Kindle or Kindle app, you're going to need an Amazon account.

Ok, first download the digital *Explorer* from the link that was sent to you. The link will look something like this:

https://www.dropbox.com/scl/fi/
fcrsosvfrvs0wnbtjwkj8/ZG_Explorer_Vol_8-
4_November_2023_s.pdf?
rlkey=3da6av23dzx7sbieu4srhu0c5&dl=0

Save it to a location on your PC where you can easily find it. Windows might want to save it to Documents or Downloads by default. Or you might prefer to save it how you organize all of your own documents. (All you Mac folks are on your own – I don't know where Apple will want to save it). Remember where it was saved.

Assuming that you have an Amazon account, there are multiple ways to get the digital *Explorer* onto your Kindle or the Kindle app. I'll walk you through a couple of different ways.

First, let's use a web browser. You can do this on your PC or Mac. Go to

https://www.amazon.com/sendtokindle

If you're not logged in, Amazon will need you to login. Once you get logged in you'll see this page:

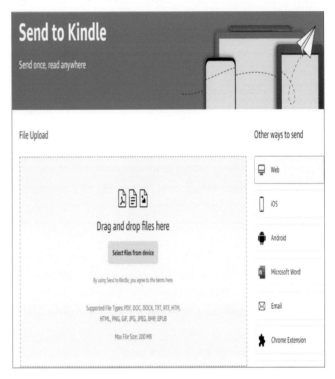

If you have a two monitor setup, put this screen on one monitor and on the other monitor bring up the folder where you downloaded and saved the digital *Explorer*; say C:/Documents, or F:/Data/*Explorer,* or wherever. Then, click on the *Explorer* file and merely drag and drop it onto the space noted above.

Or, if you prefer to not drag and drop (i.e., using a one monitor setup), click on the button above that says "Select files from Device." That will open the Windows File Explorer – navigate to where you saved the *Explorer* file, select it, then click the button to proceed.

Now you will need to wait a few minutes, but then when you go into the Kindle device or app, and look at Library, you will see the *Explorer* show up as an available title to read. When you look at the Kindle Library, the *Explorer* might not show under Books – with me, it showed up under Docs. I'm betting that all PDF files show up under Docs.

Once you click on the document to read, it will look like this (viewing it on my iPad using the Kindle app):

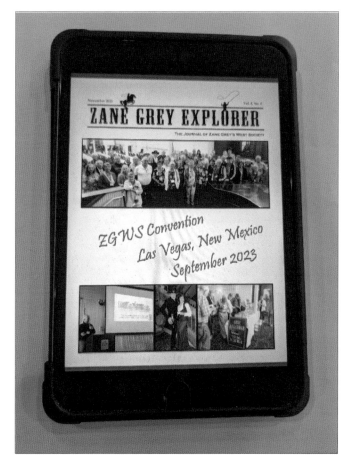

You will notice one thing from this image. Notice how the app has scaled the document to get it to fit on the screen. There aren't any formatting issues. This is really nice! If we tried to turn this into a true eBook, we would be fighting with formatting issues constantly. Using a PDF solves that issue. This image is from my iPad mini – approximately an 8" screen. I can read the document on this screen size easily. On a smartphone you would be able to pinch and zoom in to make the text larger. On a Kindle you can adjust the text size to whatever you prefer.

Now, let me point you to some other ways of getting the *Explorer* to your Kindle. Go back to the image for "Send to Kindle." Notice on the right hand side – other ways to send. It shows Web (which is what we used in the example above) but it also shows iOS, Android, Microsoft Word, Email, a Google Chrome extension, and Windows and

Mac apps. I won't go into those – with one exception — as you can follow the instructions there just as easily as I can relate them again.

The one exception is sending via email. I want to highlight that. Once you set this up, it is an extremely simple and effective way of sending the *Explorer* to your Kindle library. However, there is one caveat with this. I don't see where Amazon has a size limit on attachments to send to Kindle but I'm betting your email provider does. For example, in my case, I can't send attachments larger than 18 MB. Well, many of our *Explorers* are right in that range – 15MB to 20 MB. You might not be able to use this method for the larger *Explorers*.

Instructions for reading the digital Explorer on your B&N Nook or in the Nook app. (OR NOT!)

Remember when I suggested earlier that if you didn't already own a Barnes & Noble Nook device, go with Kindle rather than the Nook? I'm doubling down on that comment.

I found instructions online on how to download a PDF document directly to a Nook device. Earlier, I had mentioned that Bobbie used a Nook device. However, it is a much older Nook device (she has since started using our iPad mini as well). I used the Nook instructions and was able to import the *Explorer* onto the device. Then, I navigated to Documents and tried to open it. I got an error message saying something had gone wrong and the desired action could not be completed. I messed around with it a bit then gave up. I also found a post online that stated that there was no way to use the Nook app (for example, on my iPad) to read PDFs. In addition, Barnes & Noble discontinued their Nook app for Windows. So, you can't do anything from your PC's browser with a Nook device.

So . . .

To me, it just looks like B&N is not planning on supporting the Nook devices long term. They are way behind Kindle and don't seem to have any interest in catching up. If you own a Nook device, find the instructions online and see if it works for you. If not, try contacting B&N Nook support.

If you don't own a Nook, my suggestion is to go with either the Kindle app for Windows (or Mac) and use an actual Kindle device. Or go with an iPad or Android tablet and download the Kindle app (this is what I do). The Kindle process is very nice.

There are other PDF reading apps you can download for an iPad or Android tablet that I read positive reviews on, so you could also consider those. Just do a search. Also, I have read very positive reviews about the Kobo eReader devices.

How to find FREE Zane Grey eBooks

Now that you've taken the plunge into reading your digital *Explorer*, you can also read many other eBooks. Amazon has almost any book you want available as a Kindle book. There are also multiple other online sites that sell eBooks, so you can take advantage of those as well. But, you can also find many Zane Grey eBooks as free downloads, including from Kindle (Amazon).

Just go into your Amazon account, then in the search bar, type in "kindle eBooks zane grey free." Multiple titles will be listed. Be a bit careful and look at the prices, and make sure they don't require a free trial of Kindle Unlimited.

For example, I found the following titles for $0:
> The Light of Western Stars
> The Heritage of the Desert
> Wildfire
> The Man of the Forest
> The Lone Star Ranger
> The Young Forester
> The Day of the Beast
> The Border Legion
> The Mysterious Rider
> Desert Gold
> The Call of the Canyon
> The Young Lion Hunter
> The Short Stop

Many more titles (not in the public domain) are available for a dollar or less. Since I was in there, I went ahead and downloaded several of the free titles to my Kindle account. Here you can see several of the titles I downloaded in My Library on the Kindle app:

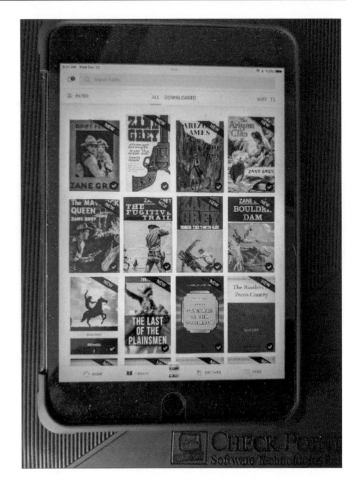

Another good source for Zane Grey eBooks (and many other authors, for that matter) is Project Gutenberg (www.gutenberg.org). Project Gutenberg, organized by Google, has a library of over seventy thousand free eBooks. These are typically books in the Public Domain. Go to the website, do a search on "zane grey" and you will see thirty-four titles listed. Project Gutenberg offers multiple formats for download – html, EPUB3 (which includes Send to Kindle), Kindle, and text. If you want a PDF copy, download the Text version, then use Microsoft Word to Export to PDF.

There are many more sites online where you can find Zane Grey material as well, from electronic books to audio books and much more.

How to make your own Zane Grey eBooks

Ok, let's say that you want a Zane Grey (or other) book that is NOT in the Public Domain, and you can't find an eBook of this title anywhere online, yet you want the title as an eBook. There is a way to make your own eBook!

Disclaimer: If a book is not in the Public Domain, you have the right to create your own digital copy for your own personal use. However, this is a very "gray" area (pun intended), so be careful. If you make your own digital copy, make sure you don't try to distribute it anywhere (especially for a fee) – and don't give a copy to all your ZGWS friends.

The way you do this is by taking a print copy of the book – hardcover or softcover – and scanning the book into a PDF format. There are two ways of doing this – both are going to destroy the book, so I recommend finding a poor copy of the title to use – the binding can be bad, you just want the paper pages to be good.

First, if you have the proper equipment, you can do this yourself fairly easily. The proper equipment consists of a high speed scanner, such as the Fujitsu line of ScanSnap scanners. However, these are a bit expensive so most people won't own one of these. You could also do this with a flatbed, all in one printer, that includes scanning capability, but it will be very tedious. The first thing you would do is cut off the spine of the book and "release" the pages from the book. Then, you run the pages through the scanner in order, creating a full blown PDF book. But, if you don't have a high speed scanner, let me propose a different option.

Second, there is a service – www.1dollarscan.com – where you can send your book and they will scan it for you. Just recognize that due to legality issues, they will not return the actual printed book to you (actually, they can for public domain books but it's pricy) – you will only receive the digital file. So, again, I recommend that you send them a book where the binding is in poor condition but has good pages (because they are also going to remove the spine and destroy the book). The book can be hardcover or paperback.

From a pricing standpoint, they used to be $1 per set (hence, 1dollarscan) for basic scanning (I'll explain a "set" in a minute) but like everything else, they have had to increase pricing to $1.20 per set. Ok, what is a set? A set is one hundred pages. So, a book with three hundred sixty pages will be four sets (you round up to the next set).

That book would then cost you $4.80 to scan plus your shipping cost to them. The output will be a file that you download from their site. www.1dollarscan has lots of other options that can increase the cost – just pay attention to those options – they can add lots of cost but you might want some of the options. They can scan magazines also.

Other Society Digital Content

Another membership benefit that will come with our measured move to digital is that we will be providing additional digital content, along with the *Explorer*. For example, we can provide full Zane Grey ebooks (those that are in the public domain). We're hoping to provide *Wanderer of the Wasteland* digitally to members before the annual convention in October. We will also be able to highlight past issues of ZGWS journals and provide past issues. Grey also wrote quite a few non-fiction magazine articles that were published nowhere else – we have plans to provide some of those digitally as well.

Summary

Ok, there you have it. I wanted to provide some insight into how you as a member can deal with digital *Explorer*s (and Zane Grey eBooks, and other electronic content). I know that many of you still want paper, but as part of the Print Plus membership, we're going to send you the digital copy of the *Explorer* anyway. Please take a look at a digital *Explorer* sometime based upon the comments I've made above – you might find that you really like having the digital Explorer!

Here is a link you can use to experiment with any of the options above:

https://www.dropbox.com/scl/fi/
fcrsosvfrvs0wnbtjwkj8/ZG_Explorer_Vol_8-
4_November_2023_s.pdf?
rlkey=3da6av23dzx7sbieu4srhu0c5&dl=0

Remember, too, that we'll have indexes and user guides on our website so that specific titles, articles and themes are easy to locate.

Happy Public Domain Day!

by Terry Bolinger

Not only was January 1st New Year's Day, it is also Public Domain Day. For 2024, in the United States, formerly copyrighted works from 1928 have now entered the Public Domain. Included in those works would be the following books and stories by Zane Grey:

Nevada
Wild Horse Mesa
Don, the Story of a Lion Dog
Tales of Fresh Water Fishing

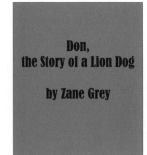

1928 was a big year for Grey with the number of books released. Most years, there are only one or two Grey titles that enter the public domain.

Public Domain means that anyone is now free to use creative works (books, songs, films, etc.) for other uses, including reprinting specific titles to sell yourself. If you look on eBay, you will see tons of pre-1928 titles by Zane Grey (and other authors) being sold by many different sellers. These sellers merely took the text of one of Grey's works, for example, and reprinted it themselves, with or without any extra material. This is perfectly legal.

One might ask if reprinting the titles makes any sense – is there really a market for such sales? While I really can't say, my first reaction is "possibly." Someone with a lot of time on their hands could generate many books based on public domain books. Quickly find the text online or scan a book yourself, convert the text to a PDF document, submit it to Amazon KDP or other alternatives, create a book cover using their Cover

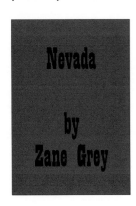

Creator, and once the project is approved, sell it on Amazon or buy a few copies yourself and list them on eBay. For a book where you can find the text online or easily scan a copy, you can probably create a sellable book in less than an hour. And the author's cost for the book is cheap – on some of these, the cost to the author might be less than $2 per copy. The author (or developer might be a better term – some folks might think of a more derogatory term for these individuals) could sell the book for $5 and make a healthy profit. Most new paperbacks these days or up in the $8 to $10 range.

Then repeat this process for hundreds of titles in the Public Domain. Even if you only sell a handful of books of each title, it adds up. Could you make a living doing this? I doubt you could get rich from this scheme but you could probably, moderately, supplement your income. Imagine there is a market where someone wants a nice clean paperback copy to read and they would love to be able to get one cheaply and conveniently. There are no shortage of book "developers" doing this that it would indicate there's some money in the idea. You could be one of them.

However, it would seem to make sense only if you could reprint hundreds if not thousands of books like this. It's a big job that may or may not ever need to be done. But if you do, please try to make better book covers than these.

So, Happy Public Domain Day!

Zane Grey's West Society is always excited when it learns that photographs from people who knew Zane Grey are made available online for fans of the great writer. Brigham Young University's L. Tom Perry Collections has announced the availability of a new collection you will all enjoy. This is the official announcement, made by Ryan Lee:

"L. Tom Perry Special Collections is pleased to announce the availability of a newly digitized collection: *Claire Wilhelm Collection on Zane Grey (MSS 8277)*. The collection contains documentation of Wilhelm's interactions with Grey while accompanying him on various expeditions. The collection contains black and white photographs of Zane Grey and his family, Claire Wilhelm and various other women on trips with Zane Grey, Native Americans, and scenes from Zane Grey movies. It also contains ephemera collected by Claire Wilhelm including silhouettes of Zane and Lina Elise Grey, a Christmas card from Zane Grey to Wilhelm, and a Zane Grey book plate. Materials date from approximately 1900 to 1956."

Here are two of the ninety images in the Claire Wilhelm Collection which can be viewed by entering *Claire Wilhelm Collection on Zane Grey (MSS 8277)* into any search engine.

Claire Wilhelm Collection Available Online

Above: The three Grey brothers (L-R) Ellsworth, R. C., Zane. Probably Lackawaxen circa 1905-1908.

Below: Secretary Claire Wilhelm and various other men and women standing in a forest holding bats and branches.

Riding the Rails to the Codroy Valley

Zane Grey and the Newfoundland Railway

by Ed Meyer

In 2022, I had the honor of publishing a "web story" in Zane Grey's West Society's public archives (ZGWS.org/archives) entitled "Zane Grey on the Rock."[1] In that publication, I was able to document in some depth the author's 1929 fishing adventures along Newfoundland's south coast. This success was largely due to a little-known article brought to my attention by our Newfoundland friends entitled "Salmon of Newfoundland," penned by Zane's brother, R. C. Grey.[2] I touched lightly on Grey's efforts to catch Atlantic salmon further to the west in the Codroy Valley, but the documentation was not nearly as strong. Grey himself only briefly stated, "I also fished the Grand Codroy on the west coast of Newfoundland, failing in this beautiful river with the dry fly."[3] Fortunately my wife Kathy recommended that we fly to Newfoundland to do more research, which we did from late August to early September in 2023. Our trip was a huge success largely because of the efforts of a wonderful watercolor painter named Clayton Hann. He opened our door to a much better understanding of Zane Grey's days along the Little Codroy and Grand Codroy Rivers. Key to our adventure was his knowledge of the role the Newfoundland Railway played in Grey's visit.

Kathy and I flew from Arizona to Deer Lake, Newfoundland, arriving on August 22, 2023. We rented a car and headed south to the Codroy Valley where we had secured a cabin for two nights. The cabin was on the Grand Codroy River not far from where it entered the Gulf of St. Lawrence. At that point, the river spread far across the valley. We were greeted with the cries of ocean-going birds and the bark of seals on a sandbar outside our cabin.

The Grand Codroy River from Meyer cabin.
(Credit: Meyer Collection).

During my previous research, I stumbled across a marvelous watercolor painting entitled "Zane Grey at Overfalls."[4] It was painted by Clayton Hann, who suggested that I call him when we arrived.

Though he lived well over three hundred miles to the northeast in Gander, Newfoundland, he had just returned to his cabin on the Codroy. Clayton is a retired diagnostic radiology physician, painter and historian. He was raised along the Newfoundland Railway where his ancestors worked for decades. Clayton documents his beloved railroad through his art. This historic passion proved invaluable to our visit.

Credit: Kalmbach Publishing Co., Bill Metzger, "Classic Trains."

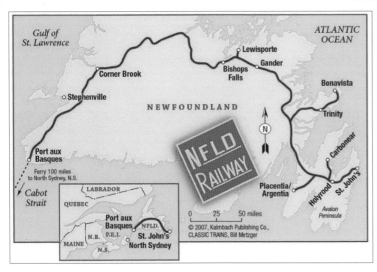

"Zane Grey at Overfalls" by Clayton Hann.

This work and others shared in this article are from Clayton Hann's published portfolio entitled "The NFLD Railway Art Exhibit."

I called Clayton soon after we arrived and he invited us to dinner where his sister, Karen Savery, welcomed us with a root vegetable salad, crab au gratin in its natural shell, steak dinner and a "cloudberry" parfait.[5] Their cabin sits on a breathtaking point overlooking the broad Grand Codroy. Before returning to our cabin, Clayton volunteered to show us places Grey visited in 1929. On the following rainy morning, Clayton and Karen's husband, Bob Savery, showed me sites on the Grand Codroy and Little Codroy Rivers tied to Zane Grey.

Tompkins

One of those locations was Tompkins, the location of the historic Afton Family Farm. I was thrilled to visit Tompkins to see if I could further document Grey's presence there. In *Newfoundland History Buffs*, John McCormick had previously described the farm. "Not only the first hunting and salmon sporting business on the west coast, but in all probability in Newfoundland . . . It was a going concern in its heyday and myself, my extended family, friends and neighbors all did our part as we were all like family . . . Zane Grey had signed the "Register" . . . I remember seeing his autograph

when I was growing up at the farm. My mother met him and it was she who showed me his autograph . . . Sadly, that register was lost when the business burnt down in 1956."

From a spot only steps from the old Tompkins railway stop, Clayton pointed out features of the Long Range Mountains shown in a 1929 Grey photograph which was clearly taken from near that spot. Following our visit, Clayton consulted with long-time Tompkins resident, Mike Aucoin, who confirmed the location of the photo and even noted that the farm shown in the valley was the old Doucette farm, now long abandoned.

Zane Grey group looking across the Little Codroy River from Tompkins, NL. (Credit: BYU, L. Tom Perry Collections, MSS8710, Box 93, File 14, Image 3918).

St. Andrews

Bob Savery and Clayton also took me to the little town of St. Andrews, only a few miles from Tompkins. Here Clayton's lifelong love for the Newfoundland Railway was invaluable. I had sent him a photo of Zane Grey with his fishing gear on a railroad "Speeder," a small vehicle used for maintenance and occasional transportation of sportsmen in Newfoundland. For many years, speeders were identified by the hand pumps used to move the vehicles. While those hand pumped vehicles still existed, the one in which Grey rode was motorized. I assumed the picture was taken near the ferry in Port aux Basques soon after Zane arrived.

Zane Grey holding flyrod on "Speeder" in Newfoundland. (Credit: BYU, L. Tom Perry Collections, MSS8710, Boz 93, File 14, Image 3895. Circle added by Ed Meyer).

"Section Crew on Speeder Near Wreckhouse". Workers are protected by a tarpaulin stretched across the speeder's front to protect from the dangerous Wreckhouse winds. (Credit: Clayton Hann, 2012).

Clayton explained that the photo of Grey and the speeder was taken at St. Andrews, not far from Tompkins. He based his conclusion on what little terrain can be seen, but also because of the two sets of railroad tracks you can see in the photo. St. Andrews was the only stop in that area with rails in that configuration.

The St. Andrews stop on the NFLD Railway. (Credit: St. Andrews 1956, Robert J. Sandusky).

The St. Andrews Station. The man in the picture is Hann's grandfather, Leander Cook, station agent at St. Andrews. (Credit: "St. Andrews Milepost 528.2," Clayton Hann, 2017).

As we stood on the old railroad right-of-way at St. Andrews,[6] we looked toward the Long Range Mountains and saw another documentation of Grey's presence in the Codroy Valley.

Left: The original Zane Grey photo. (Credit: BYU, L. Tom Perry Collections, MSS8710, Box 93, File .14, Image 3890).
Right: Current photo of the Long Range Mountains over Campbell Pond. (Photo courtesy of John Marsden).

The contours of the mountains exactly matched one of the photographs from the Zane Grey, Inc. Collection at Brigham Young University. It was a rainy day so my images are not the best, but Newfoundland friend John Marsden shared his photograph of the same location. We are looking at the Long Range Mountains towering over Campbell's Pond as seen from St. Andrews. This absolutely documents Zane Grey's presence at that location.

Overfalls

Our most exciting stop was at Overfalls, a famous Atlantic salmon fishing spot on the Grand Codroy River. This is a place I had been encouraged to visit by at least five Newfoundlanders prior to our visit because of a chimney still standing after its cabin burned many years ago. They all called it the "Zane Grey Cabin." Even though local legend is not always accurate, I could not resist the opportunity to go there.

Clayton provided me with two additional bits of information. The first was a brief quote from Kenneth Pieroway's 2013 book, *Rails Across the Rock*: "Renowned American angler Lee Wulff travelled here (Overfalls) by train and a hand-pumped railcar in 1935 to fish." While the quote did not reference Zane Grey, it did document the use of speeders to convey fishermen to Overfalls.

Ed Meyer at the Overfalls chimney.
The chimney is the only remaining piece
of what the locals refer to as
The Zane Grey Cabin.
Photo courtesy of Bob Savery, 2023.

Clayton also mentioned an old gentleman named Cyril Goodyear who had been both a Newfoundland Ranger and member of the Canadian Mounted Police who knew a lot about Zane Grey's days at Overfalls. Since our trip would take us through his hometown of Deer Lake, we hoped we could chat with him.

When we arrived at the trail to the Zane Grey Cabin at Overfalls, it soon became clear that Clayton and Bob had made advance preparations for our visit. On the day before our arrival. they had gone to the trouble of hacking a path toward the chimney and clearing brush from around the structure. As with the other places I was shown, the site was only steps away from the Newfoundland Railway right-of-way.

One concern about the site is that it may be in harm's way. Because moose are such a threat to motorists, the highway maintenance crews are clearing brush far back from the sides of the roads.

Evidently, the animals are always a risk, but especially during mating season when the bull's focus is only on the ladies rather than cars that may be driving past. Clearing will not occur at Overfalls until the summer of 2024, but the chimney may accidentally fall victim to the careless track hoes that will be doing the work. You can see the brush to be cleared crowding close behind the chimney. Zane Grey's West Society plans to communicate with the local highway supervisor to encourage caution and perhaps even discuss a possible small memorial commemorating the importance of the site.

After we visited the cabin site, Clayton asked if I would like to hike down to the river. I certainly did so we walked to where the trail headed down to the falls. Memories of dozens of similar treks from my younger day encouraged me to continue. Then I could hear my Kathy's voice shouting from inside my head, "Don't you dare!" She was right, of course, so I reluctantly passed my camera to Bob who volunteered to finish the descent and take pictures for me.

Ed Meyer and Clayton Hann at the top of the Overfalls trail. Photo courtesy of Bob Savery.

"Overfalls" (Photo courtesy of Bob Savery).

The next day, Clayton showed us places along Newfoundland's south coast that had been mentioned in Reddy Grey's *Outdoor Life* article. The day finished with dinner in a marvelous restaurant in a seaside town called Margaree. Later, Clayton dropped us off at our cabin, parting with grateful memories to last a lifetime.

However, we still wanted a stronger documentation of Zane Grey at Overfalls. When we reached Deer Lake, I called the 97-year-old Cyril Goodyear. His daughter told us he would be delighted to meet with me.

Newfoundland Ranger Cyril Goodyear.

What a delightful old gentleman! He regaled me with tales of his life with the Newfoundland Rangers and Royal Canadian Mounted Police. His adventures rivalled any of Zane Grey's own Sergeant King. (Subsequent to our adventure, the Society has sent him a copy of *King of the Royal Mounted*.) He had also served as the Deer Lake mayor, Chief Judge of the Provincial Court, Deputy Minister of Rural and Agricultural Development and much more. He is also a much-published author. When we talked about Zane Grey, his memories had faded, but he thought he might have written about Grey in one of his books. I left his home feeling honored to have met him.

When I returned home to Arizona, I decided to look up Cyril's books and there were many. *The Road to Nowhere, Against the Elements: Surviving in Newfoundland, Judging the Courts, Sometimes I Forget, Nunatsuak* and more. They are now out of print, but I did locate a copy of *Nunatsuak* and was able to view the table of contents. There I hit paydirt with an article he had written for the *St. John's Evening Telegram* in 1986/87 entitled "Zane Grey's Cabin." I ordered the book; when it arrived, I turned to that chapter where I immediately saw a picture of the same chimney I have visited. Enjoy the following excerpt from that story drawn from Mr. Goodyear's service as a Newfoundland Ranger in the Codroy Valley in 1948-1949:

"Travel by horse and sleigh was a slow process; especially when the Ranger had to stop at numerous places to do his work. As a result, we would stop overnight at one of the farms. One of my favorite places was Uncle Mike McIsaac's at Upper Ferry . . . I always enjoyed staying there as the food was excellent, the atmosphere cozy, and the District Nurse boarded there . . . One stormy evening, we were sitting by the blazing stove having a grand chat . . . It is difficult to remember now how it came up, but someone must have mentioned reading, and then we talked about western novels, and I said how much I enjoyed Zane Grey. Uncle Mike showed obvious interest and said, 'You won't believe it, but I knew Zane Grey.' I was now all ears and asked him how it came about. He told me that he used to guide foreign sportsmen when he was young, and had been Zane Grey's guide many times. He said Grey had a cabin at the Overfalls Pool on the Great Codroy River. When I said that I understood Grey had been a good outdoorsman, Uncle Mike told us that as a guide, he rarely had to do anything except be there. He said Zane Grey could do anything that was required, and enjoyed looking after himself; he was a real sportsman and not at all like many who came there. You can appreciate why that evening has remained in my memory all those years."[7]

Our trip to Newfoundland shouted out to me something about researching Zane Grey's past. Sometimes we discount folklore and personal accounts about the great author, relying only on Grey's own words or his old photographs. I believe that when we do so, we miss out on learning more about the author for whom *Zane Grey's West Society* was established. It is a lot of work doing first hand research, but the rewards are considerable. Most of all, Kathy and I will always remember Newfoundland's beauty and the heartwarming reception we received from the people we met on the "Rock."

Notes:

[1] http://www.zgws.org/archives/exhibits/show/zanegreynl/zgreynl

[2] Grey, R.C., "Salmon of Newfoundland," *Outdoor Life*, (October/November 1932)

[3] Grey, Zane, "The Madness of the Game", *Fly Fisherman*, (Volume 8, Number 3, 1977)

[4] Watercolors by Clayton Hann in this article are shared in his tribute to the Newfoundland Railway, The NFLD Railway Art Exhibit , a booklet he graciously sent me prior to our trip.

[5] Root vegetable salad, crab au gratin in its natural shell and cloudberry parfait are a few of the unique authentic Newfoundland dishes that delighted us during our visit. Sadly, we didn't experience the Rock's cod tongue though wonderful cod dinners met us at every turn.

[6] Sadly, the railway was officially abandoned on October 1, 1988. Almost all the tracks have now been removed. Sections of the original railroad bed are now a scenic ATV trail. When the railway ceased to exist, the provincial government took over the railbed and created a linear park, 547 miles long and named it the Newfoundland T'Railway Provincial Park.

[7] Goodyear, Cyril, *Nunatsuak: Stories of the Big Land- Labrador and Newfoundland* (Creative Publishers, St. Johns) 2010.

Editor's Note:

Zane Grey was famous for traveling the world, yet his multiple travels to eastern Canada are relatively unknown and undocumented, probably because he never wrote about the region in his fictional stories.

We know that he visited Newfoundland once. He stayed for about two months and visited several other areas along Newfoundland's French (south) coast. Those places included the Burnt Islands, Grandy's Brook, Grey River, Burgeo, Port aux Basques, the Bay du Nord river and Belleoram.

Some of Zane Grey's Newfoundland explorations have inspired and are integrated by Ed Meyer into a web story on the ZGWS Archives titled "Zane Grey on the Rock" and his new fiction project, a novella entitled A Gift from Muin, *which is now available on Amazon.*

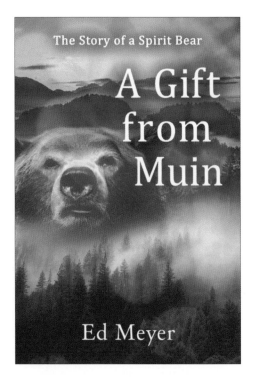

The Story of a Spirit Bear

A Gift from Muin

Ed Meyer

Grey also spent some time in Nova Scotia when he found and purchased his first large fishing yacht, "The Fisherman"; this purchase was covered in some detail by Peter Grenfell in our first two issues of the Explorer *back in 2016. We hope to present further documentation of his Nova Scotia travels in future issues.*

Buffalo Jones: Sharing a Journey of Discovery (Part One)

by Douglas Adams

I'd like to take a few moments to share an incredible journey of discovery I currently find myself undertaking. This journey was never planned and began in a very unexpected way. Although far from complete, the story that is unfolding before my eyes is simply an amazing tale of American History. When I was given the chance to present to Zane Grey's West Society in Las Vegas, New Mexico, at the 2023 annual convention I was quite honored, especially since my Uncle Todd Whitmer was there with me. This is a portion of that presentation.

The Adams' Family
The Author Doug (Right) & his Father Don (Left)

The Phone Call

This all began with a phone call in late 2018. My father called me in the evening after work and the conversation began in the usual way. "Hi Pop!" "What's up?" I asked. "Well Doug," my dad answered, "I found out who my real father was." His name was Charles Whitmer. This was quite a family revelation. My father had been told only after my grandmother passed away in 1993 that the man he called father throughout his childhood, George Adams, was not his natural father. George had adopted my dad when he married my grandmother when my dad was only two years old. This family secret was kept from my dad all this time. Unfortunately, we were not given any other details or names that helped our search. For a quarter-century we tried and found nothing to help us determine the pieces to this mysterious part of our family lineage. But the Christmas prior, my mother gifted my dad a DNA testing kit. Initially the results showed no close matches, but that had just changed. My dad continued our conversation: "I have a younger brother (Todd Whitmer) and sister" (Lin Martin) my dad said. This was exciting news!

My great, great, grandfather: C. J. "Buffalo" Jones.
Photo courtesy of Douglas Adams.

The two brothers meet for the first time

Don Adams 86 years old (left)
and
Todd Whitmer 70 Years old (right)

2018

Not only were some of the lingering questions about his childhood being answered, but my dad is all about family. And our family just got bigger. We couldn't wait to meet them! But as chance would have it, this conversation was far from over. My dad continued: "There's more" he said. "Our family is from Kansas." Now this was a shock! Everyone on both sides of my family is from the same area in South Central Pennsylvania. The thought of our family tree having roots in far away Kansas took a few minutes to comprehend. As I was still working on grasping the Kansas implications, my dad dropped the real bombshell. "Go to your computer and look up Buffalo Jones." So, at my dad's request, I searched for the man with that somewhat odd nickname. As the results came up on the computer screen, I remember asking my dad in a nonchalant way, "Okay dad, who's this cat?" "Why, that's your great, great grandfather," came the answer. Needless to say, this was a good day for our family.

Most times when you reach a crossroads in your life, you at least can see or sense the change coming. But it this case, an unexpected five-minute phone call totally altered the course of my life's future focus, and set in motion a journey to truly understand this strange and unfamiliar family lineage. Not only was there new family to meet and

get to know, there was this incredible legacy of Buffalo Jones that came with this revelation to understand. I spent the next few days looking over the seemly endless accomplishments of this Jones fellow. Preserver of the buffalo, Arctic explorer, buffalo hunter, Game Warden of Yellowstone, friend of Teddy Roosevelt and Buffalo Bill, roper of mountain lions and rhinos, an inspiration to famed western writer Zane Grey, and more. That was one name that jumped out at me right away. As fast as I could get my hands on the book *Roping Lions in the Grand Canyon*, I was on my way to my personal journey of discovery. A journey that is leading me to not only to piece together new and exciting elements of true American history and western lore, but to the literal edges of lonely and dangerous cliffs and mind-blowing purple prose western sunsets. It is part of this on-going journey that I'd like to share with you now.

The Zane Grey – "Buffalo" Jones Connection

On February 17th, 1921, a reflective Zane Grey sat down to write a letter to Olive Jones-Whitmer of Topeka, Kansas. Ollie, as she was known to her friends, was the oldest surviving daughter of the nationally famous adventurer and showman "Buffalo" Jones. Her father had passed away nearly sixteen months prior at the age of 75. In his letter Grey took a moment to openly express his true feelings for the old buckskin hunter and plainsman he had met and shared incredibly unique and thrilling adventures with some fourteen years previously.

"I am a dreamer, ... I loved and idealized your father; I loved the idea of owing my start to one whom I conceived to be a great pioneer and to whom I, by my writings help bring the recognition due him."

Zane Grey.

Letter to Olive Whitmer, Feb 17th, 1921

Zane wrote:

"I am a dreamer, . . . I loved and idealized your father; I loved the idea of owing my start to one whom I conceived to be a great pioneer and to whom I, by my writings, help bring the recognition due him."

At the time this letter was typed, Zane Grey was a leading and internationally renowned author with millions of books sold and at the height of his success. His now well-established formula of complex heroes and heroines, thrilling twists, descriptions of stunning western vistas mixed with romance and a romantic view of the western lifestyle had cemented the core outline that so many fictional novels, stories and movies of the western genre would follow for decades to come. The name of "Buffalo" Jones was also nationally well-remembered for his worldwide exploits with wild animals. And most importantly of all, he was credited as one of the main influences in the preservation of his beloved American buffalo by the American Bison Society.

Yet the fortunes of both men were very different in the final days of 1906 when Alvah James introduced the two men after one of Jones' movie and lecture presentations he annually preformed in New York. Jones, with his ever-flamboyant style, had just suffered through a largely disbelieving audience that openly challenged his seemingly far-fetched stories of arctic wolf encounters and live capture tales of full-grown wild cougars and grizzly bears. There were calls of "liar" and "faker" during his presentation. These insults were largely attributed to a group of men for the exclusive Camp Fire Club of New York that had traveled to Brooklyn to see his performance. These accusations were leveled despite the fact Jones had some of the first action moving motion pictures and stereographic photographs ever seen of these animals in the wild to back up his narratives. Conversely, sitting almost completely anonymous to anyone in the audience, Doctor Pearl Zane Grey, a frustrated dentist and struggling would-be writer who just couldn't seem to find that breakthrough manuscript or writing formula, sat and watched the whole debacle. As is so often the case, neither Jones nor Grey could have possibly imagined that would happen next would change not only the course of both their lives, but alter the way the mystique of the American West would forever be remembered. So, to better comprehend this crossroads event in literary American history, let's examine the question, Who was "Buffalo" Jones?

Who was Charles Jesse "Buffalo" Jones?

Charlie Jones was born into a large family in 1842 just outside Bloomington, Illinois. His father, Noah Nichol Jones, had emigrated from Massachusetts. Noah in his teenage years stopped along the way to work on the Mississippi water course in the "Tom Sawyer" era on the river. His middle name of Nichol was in honor of his mother's family which boasted a heavy Pilgrim ancestry.

Charley Jones   C. J. Jones   Buffalo Jones   Colonel Jones

But Charley's father arrived too late on the Illinois frontier to receive a full land grant from the government. With all the free land spoken for, he was forced to purchase three small and divided plots of land at auction. Farming three plots that were some distance apart was not easy. Charlie simply remembered this time as living in "a sweat box" with all the hard work his father demanded. It wasn't until Charley was in his mid-teens that Noah saved enough money to buy a single large farm in the town of Normal, Illinois. In Charlie's youth, instead of playing games like other children, his spare time was spent pouring over several of his favorite books and hunting. Thoughts of encountering exotic animals, following in the footsteps of arctic explorers and other heroic adventure filled his dreams. In a yearning that could only be described as "be careful what you wish for," one of Charlie's biggest daydreams was to be locked in a desperate fight to the death with ravenous Russian wolves, as described in the books he read.

In time, his father developed a reputation as a thrifty farmer, and a most persistent and shrewd trader, as well as an excellent breeder of mules. In order to distinguish himself from the hundreds of other Joneses in the area, Noah Jones adopted the catchy business nickname of "Yankee" Jones in honor of his Massachusetts birthplace.

Charley would ultimately spend two years in college before, as he put it, "he could break free from his father." Having watched his father work for years until he had a large farm of his own, he looked west to the new state of Kansas and its seemly endless open landscape and unlimited wild game. There was a plethora of land for the taking in Kansas. Although known for several devastating droughts in the early years, there was also a dream of Kansas that attracted so many young adults from large families in mid-western states. Kansas was never short on sunshine, and when the rains came at the right times, the bounty was second to none.

Worrall's "Drouthy Kansas" painting made a whimsical statement on the state's negative image.

Henry Worrall

So, with a pocket full of Osage Orange seeds and little else, Charley headed west and ended up in Troy, Kansas in the northeastern tip of the state just across the Missouri River. His plan was to open a nursery where his Osage Orange shrubs in bulk could be sold as a hedge substitute for wooded fencing on the hundreds of farms springing up all around the area. With little to no trees on the open plains to supply wooded fences, the idea seemed to be a very good one. With fruit tree saplings imported from Charley's friends back in Illinois, he found some early financial success and his nursery became a well-known place in Troy. And with the success of his business, Charley Jones became known as locally as C. J. Jones.

C. J. had a girl back home in Illinois that he hoped to win his fortune and woo her out west with him, but that all changed one night at a dance in town. That night he met Martha "Mattie" J. Walton. Mattie quickly became the love of C. J.'s life and they were soon married. Not only would Mattie stand by her man through incredibly difficult and often lonely times, but her family name also came with a legacy that would greatly influence C. J. in his later years. The Waltons could trace their lineage directly back to Sir Isaak Walton in 1650's England. Walton, who was an avid fisherman, had written a book known as *The Compleat Angler* which contained a revolutionary concept. If you want to enjoy fishing, you must protect the environment in which the fish thrives. This book was considered one of the most important books in environmental history. The problem was, the concept of conservation was far from anybody's mind during the rapid expansion into the untamed American West.

Although C. J. worked very hard and his business was successful, there were signs of a coming storm on the eastern great plains — a pattern of destruction that worried anyone that relied on agriculture and farming for a living. It was said that if you "show me a successfully farmer, and I'll show you a successful crop of grasshoppers."

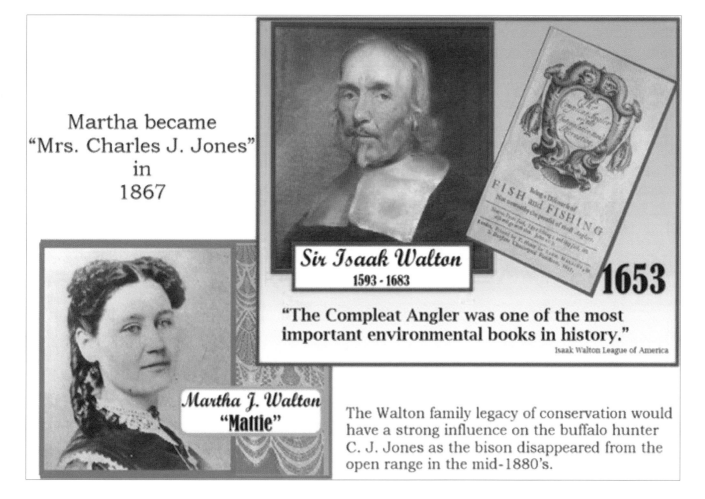

Martha became
"Mrs. Charles J. Jones"
in
1867

Sir Isaak Walton
1593 - 1683

1653

Martha J. Walton
"**Mattie**"

"The Compleat Angler was one of the most important environmental books in history."
Isaak Walton League of America

The Walton family legacy of conservation would have a strong influence on the buffalo hunter C. J. Jones as the bison disappeared from the open range in the mid-1880's.

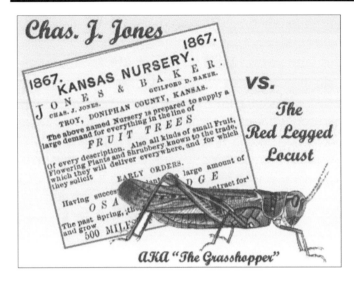

Hatching out in April, many farmers would find their crops destroyed before the local locusts matured and flew away in the early part of July. Often, after the grasshoppers left there was time to resow some crops to salvage part of the season.

However, there was something much more ominous that was occurring more frequently as the years passed. Far out on the western plains where the railroad was building their long lonely routes across the plains to the Rocky Mountains, came reports of black swarms of locusts flying high above, coming from somewhere to the northwest. These late-arriving locusts landed in the eastern part of Kansas just after the spring, grasshoppers having recently departed in late July. Their arrival was absolutely devastating to the remaining crops. These red-legged pests were known as the Rocky Mountain Locusts. Their numbers and the devastation they wrought were increasing every year. Not only were the grasshoppers destroying C. J.'s inventory of plants, but no one would invest money in plants that were likely to be destroyed by the grasshopper plague in short order.

The Soddie

After four years of moderate success in the nursery business, C. J. realized he wouldn't be able to outlast the grasshoppers and closed up shop, openly admitting that he had been beaten by the locusts.

Leaving the relative comfort of Troy, Jones and his wife traveled west by wagon to a very nice parcel of land he had secured out in the north central part of Kansas frontier along a little bend in the South Solomon River. However, sod busting and starting up a farm was not an easy task. For his wife Mattie, who had grown up in LaPorte, Indiana, living on the western edge of civilization was a very difficult adjustment and far from the comfort of big town living. And living in a house made of sod (known as Soddies) comes with its own challenges. The work was hard during the planting and harvesting season, but there was very little to do on an open plains farm in the wintertime except feed the livestock. So, when many of the local farmers approached C. J. with an offer to make significant money through the cold windy days of a Kansas winter, he gladly accepted the opportunity.

The year was 1871 and a process had just been refined for taking buffalo hides and converting them into heavy-grade leather for military equipment used by European armies, as well as belts to drive the steam driven machines of the eastern industrial factories. Until that time, the buffalo was mainly only hunted for its meat, while a few of their hides were converted into "buffalo robes" by a long time-consuming tanning process used by Native American tribes.

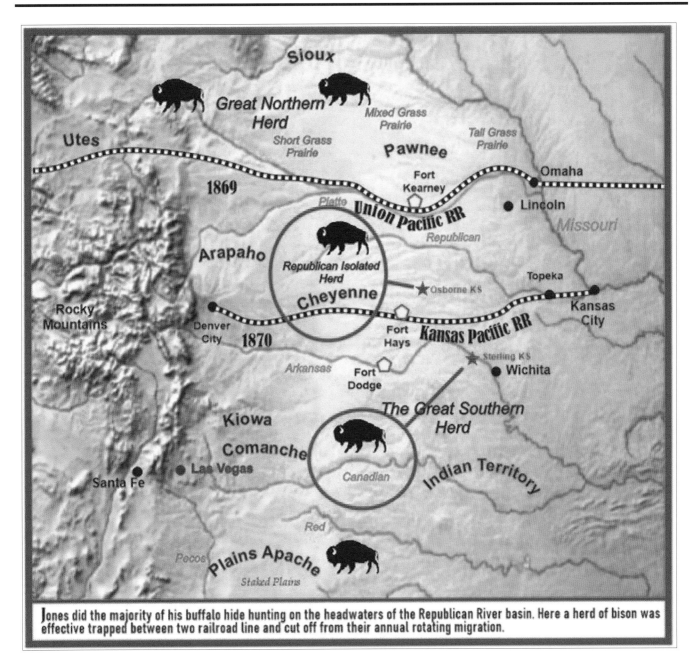

Jones did the majority of his buffalo hide hunting on the headwaters of the Republican River basin. Here a herd of bison was effective trapped between two railroad line and cut off from their annual rotating migration.

Since C. J. was a very good long-range shot with his rifle, a local collection of famers offered him a very attractive wage of .50 cents per buffalo he dropped. The rest of the group would skin and deliver to market the hides where they received between $1.50 to $3.50 per hide depending on the size and quality.

So, for several years, Jones would hunt bison on the high plains of the Republican River headwaters in western Kansas and eastern Colorado when not working on his farm in order to supplement the family income. Since the buffalo hide hunting business proved far more lucrative than farming, Jones shifted his focus spending more time hunting than turning dirt.

The environment on the high plains near the Rocky Mountains was, at that time, one of the deadliest on Earth. A land of very little shelter and drastically changing weather, winter hunting was a deadly prospect for the unprepared. Jones was hunting in what was the traditional hunting grounds of the Cheyenne and Arapaho Native American tribes. The destruction of their primary food source was a source of great distress to the great warrior nations.

Sharps "Big 50" Rifle

In addition, raiding parties of rival tribes such the Pawnee, Sioux, Utes and Comanche made any encounters with the natives a very dangerous venture. But at the heart of the trouble lie the renegade profiteers that stole, ransacked, and often murdered individuals they came across for their trappings. These unscrupulous white men raided the local tribes for their horses, sold whiskey and guns for hides, and generally took advantage of anyone in a weaker position than themselves.

When coming across another group on the open plains, the unwritten rule at that time was this: if your strength was equal to the other party you encountered, you looked to trade. If your party held a strength (or numbers) advantage, you looked to take advantage of the weaker party. And if you found yourself in a position of disadvantage, beware for you, and you dare not show weakness.

Since Jones was the shooter in his outfit, he would rise before dawn and head out on the open prairie alone to stalk his quarry. Having to be ever vigilant, if caught out in the open by an approaching group of men, the universal sign to take heed and do not approach was for the hunter/shooter to stand up for all to see and hold their long-range Sharp's rifle high over his head.

This signaled their intent not to allow the stronger group to approach within Winchester, pistol, and arrow range where an approaching party's numbers gave them a clear-cut advantage. According to Jones, if the stronger party still advanced, a few shots over their heads and landing nearby was usually enough to persuade them to change their course and pass him by. It was this stand alone, never show fear or weakness attitude that C. J. would carry through the remainder of his days, in both the wilderness and in his future business dealings.

While on the hunting grounds, it was common for the hunters to give nicknames to places and persons in order to distinguish them from others. The one caveat about this nicknaming tradition was you don't often get to choose your own nickname. That right usually went to the wily old veterans. There were a lot of Joneses on the range. But not too many of them were college boys. Jones was an acute observer and watched the bison, noting every detail of the animal's behavior. One common observation about C. J. throughout his life was that he talked a lot, no doubt sounding like an expert on the bison's habits. Hence the title of "Buffalo" Jones was bestowed on him while he was out on the prairie. This was a name he was not personally very fond of, but was given, nonetheless.

The hide hunting of the buffalo was a profitable endeavor for Jones, but it soon became a burden for him as well. The growing senselessness of the bison slaughter bothered him a great deal. Looking into the eyes of so many beasts as they died began to change his attitude. He felt that he wanted to do something for the bison, but at the time he didn't know what. Many nights after the day slaughter he wanted throw away his rifle and quit.

The Universal Sign to Stay Away.

But the threat to others of his long-range rifle was the only thing keeping him alive. Finally, he did break his rifle over a wagon wheel and packed up his family and moved back to Emporia, Kansas.

Back in eastern Kansas C. J. Jones landed a very sought-after job as a Mail Route Agent for the Atchison, Topeka and Santa Fe Railroad. Working on the new rail line that extended past Dodge City, Kansas and into Colorado was a very important position. His time there coincided with the legendary Wyatt Earp / Bat Masterson days in Dodge City. One day when the train was just past Dodge City, a herd of buffalo stopped the train as they roamed. This was a common occurrence at that time.

C. J. jumped off the train with a rifle determined to get a buffalo for the meat. Not realizing that Jones was off the train, the conductor signaled the engineer to continue after the buffalo cleared the tracks, and they left Jones alone on the prairie. Not only did Jones have to wait till the next day's train came by to get home, he had left the Mail Car unlocked and open. This was a mistake for which he would eventually lose his job.

When he did return, those he considered enemies began to spitefully call him "Buffalo" Jones to remind him of his folly and the beast he had pursued.

Never to be thwarted, C. J.'s next effort was to promote shows and competitions. He sponsored a Sunday School Jubilee setting up cheap train fares to bring in people from all over. The Jubilee was a great success. He made more money in one day than anyone in town not associated with the railroad did in a year. Afterwards, C. J. decided to go bigger and better so he set up what he termed "The Great Buffalo Hunt" in Topeka. And as he was advertising his Great Buffalo Hunt show in the newspapers, the common question arose from the eastern Kansas town folk was: Who is C. J. Jones? "Never heard of him before" came the responses. So, even though the moniker "Buffalo" Jones had been often used in the past in an unflattering way, Charles Jesse Jones finally relented and embraced his long-time nickname by adopting the business and showman title of "Buffalo" Jones to distinguish himself from all the other Joneses, just as his father had with "Yankee" Jones back in Illinois.

This is a tale to be continued . . .

A. T. & Santa Fe Rail Road
Mail Route Agent

November 18th, 1874

C. J. Jones, route agent on the Atchison, Topeka and Santa Fe, is reported by the Newton *Kansan* as having jumped off his mail car, leaving it open, and, gun in hand, chased the buffalo over the plains. This occurred just west of Dodge city. The train left him to be picked up by the next.
Topeka Record.

Hey, There goes "Buffalo" Jones!

AI (Specifically ChatGPT): Blessing or Menace? Probably Both.

by Robert J. Lentz, Terry Bolinger, Ed Meyer and *David G. Simpson*

Over the past months some of our noted ZGWS members have conducted an email discussion about the very public arrival of AI: Artificial Intelligence, in terms of its advantages, disadvantages, benefits, dangers and effects on groups like our own. I was witness to this exchange of ideas, opinions and warnings, but I confess that I did not add anything to the discussion. Not because I didn't care, but because I don't have a handle on the situation. Not having much of an opinion either way, I didn't feel secure offering any thoughts about the emergence of this writing aid, one which promises to boost the grammatical and technical prowess of anyone who uses it, but also one which can be seen as a replacement to actual literacy.

Truthfully, I still don't really know what I personally think about it. I don't see myself ever using ChatGPT or any other writing aid which might suggest different wording, punctuation, grammar or syntax to help make me appear to be better, or smarter, than I am. And yet, what is wrong with that goal? I refer to a dictionary now and then, and a thesaurus, too. I don't bother with more complex writing tools, but that's more because I am lazy than reticent. If a writing tool exists to aid in tasks such as writing and editing this journal, why would I hesitate to use it? It might make me a much better writer and editor.

It's because I am a science-fiction guy. I know all too well that one thing will lead to another and word changing will lead to paragraph changing and document changing and soon the robots will be running the world. I've seen *Colossus: The Forbin Project* and I've seen *The Terminator* and its ilk and I know where this ends. The question isn't if the Artificial Intelligence will take over, but when. I'm hoping that I will have had a nice long life and not be around anymore when that occurs.

But hey, in the meantime, we have to deal with this new technology that anybody can utilize to easily improve their writing skills.

Why so much fuss, you might ask? I'll let Terry Bolinger explain, as he did in a March 2 email:

By now, many of you might have heard about ChatGPT. "ChatGPT, the general-purpose AI chatbot prototype that the internet is obsessed with right now, has taken the world by storm over the past few months. It's quickly become the dominant example of the influence AI-generated content will have in the future, showing just how powerful these tools can be. It's made by OpenAI, well-known for having developed the text-to-image generator DALL-E, and it's currently available for anyone to try out for free."

I decided to try my hand at using ChatGPT, and it's scary and it's simple. I accessed the online website and made this query:

"write a four-paragraph essay explaining why Zane Grey is the most popular western fiction author of all time and include one photo of Zane Grey".

Here is the output I received from ChatGPT:

"Zane Grey is widely considered the most popular western fiction author of all time. Born in Zanesville, Ohio, in 1872, Grey was an avid outdoorsman and fisherman from an early age. He used his love of the American West to create some of the most vivid and compelling portrayals of cowboy life in his books. His writing was characterized by its authenticity, as Grey often based his stories on his own experiences and extensive research.

Grey's popularity began in the early 1900s with the publication of his first novel, "Betty Zane," a historical novel based on his ancestor's role in the American Revolution. He went on to write dozens of novels over the course of his career, including "Riders of the Purple Sage," "The Lone Star Ranger," and "Wildfire." His books were filled with action, adventure, and romance, and he became known for his ability to transport readers to the rugged landscapes and wild frontier towns of the American West.

Grey's success as a writer was due in part to his ability to tap into the American fascination with the Western frontier. His books were incredibly popular in the early 20th century and were widely read by both men and women. He became known as the "Father of the Western," and his influence can be seen in the work of many later writers, including Louis L'Amour and Cormac McCarthy.

In addition to his writing, Grey was also an accomplished fisherman and conservationist. He used his writing to promote the protection of natural resources, and his books often featured descriptions of the beauty and grandeur of the American West. Today, Grey's books continue to be read and loved by fans of Western fiction all over the world, cementing his place as one of the most beloved authors of all time."

Editor's Note: The link for the photo did not work for me, so I cannot include it here. But it is clear that the software utilized to create that description of Zane Grey's career did what it was designed to do, and rather well. It hits several of Grey's career highlights and presents an overall picture of the author that is not only accurate but even seems hyperbolic enough to be written by a fan. But note that no sources are referenced and the "Betty Zane" description is not quite as accurate as the rest of this synopsis. Now, back to Terry's take:

Terry Bolinger

Those of you that still have ties into academia are well aware of ChatGPT, I'm sure. I've read multiple stories of students using ChatGPT to write papers for their assignments, rather than doing the papers themselves. Professors everywhere are worried about the impact of this AI tool. Supposedly there are tools that can determine if a work was AI generated or not, but I've read that they might not work too well plus they are extremely expensive.

I've read several accounts where ChatGPT edited photos and created artwork (and music and poetry) that was entered into contests and the AI generated work won the contest.

I read an article where a publishing company that publishes science fiction novels stopped accepting submissions of works as their submissions increased 10 fold almost overnight and they were able to determine that most of the submissions were generated by ChatGPT. Those works were not 4 paragraph works — they were full novels! The publishing house — who pays for accepted submissions — has put an indefinite hold on accepting submissions and is trying to determine how they're going to proceed. Apparently, most of the people submitting were trying to make a fast buck.

To reiterate — I did NOT write the above four paragraphs — ChatGPT generated this all on its own. I sat here and watched it as it typed out the paragraphs.

To some folks, this is heresy. And, it really opens up a huge can of worms. From the above, we can see where it got the photo, but we don't know where it got the text (I checked and it might have gotten some information from Wikipedia but it didn't copy it verbatim from there — this looks like an original work).

But, think of this as a very intelligent web search tool — it's pulling its information from sources on the web and then putting it together in a scholarly form. There is a concern about plagiarism, as we don't know where the information came from. This reinforces the concept that if you don't want your information to be shared, DON'T post it on the Internet. This tool will use that information indiscriminately and not worry about the legalities. It could be that government entities will eventually get involved and require that the tool provide it's sources or references (or somehow respect copyrights) but it's not there at the moment. Also, note that ChatGPT doesn't know if information is good or not — witness the comment above about Betty Zane being a historical novel based on his ancestor's role in the American Revolution.

I can see some real benefits of this technology but at the same time, there are many downsides. We should be aware of it as we will probably be impacted by it as time goes on.

That was Terry Bolinger's assessment back in March, one that set the wheels in motion for what is to come. Ed Meyer replied the next day, with his usual brevity and a much more positive outlook on this burgeoning technology:

My initial reaction is that we need to figure out how to use this technology to advance our ZGWS mission rather than look the other way and let the world pass us by as it has been doing as we have grown older as an organization. I'm thrilled that we are having this discussion and welcome the future.

Then Ed took the next step. He asked ChatGPT to concoct a literary tale about Zane Grey.

Here was my command, "Write a story no more than 1000 words about the friends Jim Emmett, a polygamist, and Zane Grey."

And here is what is really a delightful story:

Ed Meyer

"Jim Emmett had always been a bit of an oddball. He grew up in a small town in Utah, where his family was one of the few that still practiced polygamy. Jim never really fit in with the other kids at school, who always seemed to look at him with a mix of curiosity and suspicion.

But Jim didn't let that bother him. He had a small group of friends that he hung out with, and they were all just as weird as he was. One of his closest friends was a man named Zane Grey. Zane was also from a polygamous family, but he had long since left that way of life behind.

Despite their different paths, Jim and Zane remained close friends. They would often meet up at the local diner to chat over coffee and pie. It was there that Jim would sometimes share his dreams of having multiple wives, while Zane would listen and nod politely.

One day, Jim surprised Zane by telling him that he had finally found a woman who was willing to be his second wife. Zane was taken aback. He had always known that Jim was interested in polygamy, but he had never thought he would actually go through with it.

But as Jim began to talk more about his new wife, Zane realized that this wasn't just some whim. Jim was genuinely in love with this woman, and he truly believed that having multiple wives was the right path for him.

Over the next few months, Jim's relationship with his new wife grew stronger. Zane watched from the sidelines, still feeling a bit uncomfortable with the whole situation. But he could see how happy Jim was, and he didn't want to ruin their friendship by passing judgment.

Then one day, Jim dropped a bombshell on Zane. He had met yet another woman, and he wanted to take her as his third wife.

Zane was stunned. He had always thought that Jim's relationship with his second wife was a bit strange, but he had never imagined that Jim would continue to seek out more wives.

But as Jim explained his reasoning, Zane began to understand. For Jim, polygamy wasn't just about having multiple sexual partners. It was about building a community of people who loved and supported one another.

As Jim's third wife moved in with the other two, Zane found himself spending more time with the trio. He began to see how they all worked together, taking care of each other's needs and supporting each other through difficult times.

And slowly but surely, Zane began to let go of his own preconceptions about polygamy. He realized that for some people, having multiple spouses wasn't just a lifestyle choice — it was a deeply held belief.

Years went by, and Jim's family continued to grow. Zane watched as the children grew up, happy and loved by their three mothers and one father. He saw how Jim's wives worked together to create a stable and supportive environment for their family, and he couldn't help but admire their dedication and love for one another.

In the end, Zane realized that his friendship with Jim was worth more than his own beliefs about marriage and relationships. He learned that sometimes, the people we love the most are the ones who challenge us the most — and that's okay.

And so, Jim and Zane remained friends until the end of their days, united by a bond that was stronger than any disagreement about lifestyle choices or beliefs."

David G. Simpson

Note that Ed's request didn't specify any positive or negative aspect toward polygamy; only that the subject link the two friends in some way.

I am also amused because the program obviously did not connect the names of the two characters with the two real, famous people to which Ed was referring with his question. It could have been Jake and Elwood; the story would have remained the same.

A few other emails were exchanged, mostly about the growing menace from AI — it can listen to you and use your voice for anything it wants! — all of which makes me long for a simpler, realer world, but none of which triggered any stronger interest in ChatGPT. And then I met David G. Simpson.

Rosanne Vrugtman, Dan Terrick and I were at the Mid-Atlantic Nostalgia Convention (MANC) in early September, and David Simpson stopped by our ZGWS table one day. He had something he wanted to show us. I took one look at it and knew it was going to appear in this issue. But I'll let him tell the story:

I'd heard about the artificial intelligence engine ChatGPT over the past few months, but never tried it myself. After a co-worker recently demonstrated it for me, I signed up for an account, just to try it for myself.

My first experiments with ChatGPT involved asking it simple questions: "What is the capital of South Dakota?," and so forth, which it handled easily. I then began asking questions in different languages, and discovered I could ask a question in Latin, Esperanto, or even Interlingua, and it would recognize the language and respond in the same language.

I then got the idea to ask ChatGPT to do some creative writing, and randomly chose "cheeseburgers" as the topic. I started by asking it to write a haiku about cheeseburgers, and got this:

> Juicy beef sizzles,
> Melted cheese, savory bite,
> Cheeseburgers delight.

I then asked for a limerick about cheeseburgers, and it wrote this:

> There once was a juicy cheeseburger,
> With toppings that made taste buds stir.
> Bacon crispy and cheese so melty,
> Lettuce, tomato, all so tasty,
> A delight that made stomachs concur.

Then I tried something a little more challenging, and asked ChatGPT to write a poem about cheeseburgers, in the style of poet e. e. cummings (who famously dislikes capital letters). I got this:

> cheeseburgers taste
> like heaven on a bun
> juicy patty sizzles
> with each savory run
>
> lettuce dances lightly
> tomato bursts with glee
> cheese melts and embraces
> the meat in harmony

> ketchup sings a tangy tune
> mustard adds its zest
> pickles offer a crunchy note
> on this burger fest
>
> buns hold it all together
> as flavors intertwine
> a symphony of deliciousness
> in each bite divine
> oh, cheeseburgers of delight
> how you bring such cheer
> a culinary masterpiece
> to savor without fear
>
> in this burger poetry
> we celebrate your worth
> cheeseburgers, oh cheeseburgers,
> the tastiest on earth.

Next, I asked ChatGPT to write a sonnet about cheeseburgers, in the style of William Shakespeare. It did a nice job with this:

> Upon the plate, a masterpiece divine,
> A marriage of flavors, true delight found,
> Behold! The cheeseburger, treasure so fine,
> In tender bun, thy secrets are profound.
>
> The patty, seasoned well, a savory kiss,
> A symphony of spices, oh so grand,
> Its sizzling whispers fill the air with bliss,
> As flames embrace, the meat at thy command.
>
> Above, a crown of cheese, melted and golden,
> Enrobing the beef with creamy delight,
> Its richness, a sensation unsurpassed, beholden,
> A feast for taste buds, pure rapture in sight.
>
> With lettuce, tomato, and pickles bestowed,
> A cheeseburger's glory, a tale to be told.

I then moved on to short stories, starting with science fiction. I asked ChatGPT to write short stories about cheeseburgers conquering the Earth and cheeseburgers travelling through time, but the results weren't especially interesting. (Editor's note: I do find it intriguing that the stories which demand more imagination and flights of fancy are those which ChatGPT finds more difficult to perform than very specific, stylized requests. I would assume that with time, the program will be able to tackle this type of story as well).

But when I asked it to write a short story about cheeseburgers in the style of a Zane Grey Western, it produced this masterpiece:

The Cheeseburger Saloon

The sun sank low on the horizon, casting long shadows across the rugged plains of the Wild West. Dust swirled in the air, kicked up by the hooves of a lone rider making his way through the barren land. His name was Jack Callahan, a hardened cowboy with a taste for adventure and a hankering for cheeseburgers.

Jack had heard rumors of a legendary saloon tucked away in the heart of a desolate canyon, where the proprietor served the juiciest, most mouthwatering cheeseburgers west of the Mississippi. With each passing mile, his hunger grew, and the thought of sinking his teeth into a savory patty of meat, topped with gooey cheese and crispy bacon, fueled his determination.

After days of riding, Jack finally spotted the canyon on the horizon. The rocky walls rose high into the sky, forming a natural fortress that guarded the hidden treasure within. With a flick of his reins, Jack urged his trusty steed, Thunder, to a gallop, racing toward the tantalizing aroma that teased his senses.

As Jack entered the canyon, the sound of his horse's hooves echoed off the walls, creating a symphony of anticipation. He dis-

mounted and hitched Thunder to a weathered hitching post before pushing open the creaking saloon doors. The air inside was thick with the smell of tobacco and whiskey, but Jack's attention was fixed on the sizzling griddle behind the counter.

The saloon was dimly lit, its patrons hunched over tables and murmuring to each other. Jack strode up to the counter, where a grizzled bartender with a bushy mustache and a worn apron stood ready to take his order.

"Looking for something to satisfy a man's hunger," Jack drawled, his eyes fixed on the sizzling patties. "I've heard tell that you serve the finest cheeseburgers in these parts."

The bartender's eyes twinkled as he nodded. "You heard right, stranger. We got the best damn cheeseburgers this side of the Rockies. You want the works?"

Jack's mouth watered at the thought. "Load 'em up with all the fixin's, partner. I've been dreamin' of sinking my teeth into one of those juicy beauties for days."

The bartender chuckled, his hands working deftly as he assembled the perfect cheeseburger. He piled on lettuce, tomatoes, pickles, and a slather of tangy sauce, before crowning it with a generous heap of melted cheddar cheese. A side of crispy fries accompanied the masterpiece.

With trembling hands, Jack picked up the burger, feeling the warmth seep through his calloused fingers. He took a bite, and the flavors exploded in his mouth. The juicy meat, perfectly seasoned, combined with the creamy cheese and the crunch of the lettuce. It was a symphony of tastes, a moment of bliss in the rugged West.

As he savored each mouthful, the hardships of the trail faded away. The toil and sweat of the cowboy's life were forgotten, replaced by the simple pleasure of a well-cooked meal. The cheeseburger was a reminder of the small joys that made life worth living, even amidst the harsh realities of the frontier.

Jack polished off the burger, savoring the last morsel before wiping his mouth with the back of his hand. He met the bartender's gaze and nodded, a silent understanding passing between them. No words were needed; they both knew that this cheeseburger was more than just a meal—it was a symbol of hope, a respite from the trials of the West.

With a grateful nod, Jack tossed a few coins on the counter and stepped out into the fading light. As he mounted Thunder and rode off into the sunset, he carried with him the memory of that perfect cheeseburger, a taste that would forever linger on his lips, reminding him of the simple joys that could be found in the most unexpected places.

And so, the legend of the cheeseburger saloon lived on, whispered among cowboys by campfires, a tale of a place where weary souls could find solace and satisfaction in a single bite.

Now *that* is a story. It may not be vintage Zane Grey but it seems to catch the gist. If Grey had

chosen to write about a cheeseburger, or the quest to find one, his tale might have emerged in this manner. I cannot fault the poetry, either.

In the good old days, for instance in Zane Grey's era, writers were expected to mine their own (hopefully vivid) imaginations for ideas and to present their thoughts in meaningful ways that reflected their own literary training and philosophy of life. Now it seems that an algorithm can do it all in an anonymous manner, able to mimic pretty much anyone in any form about any subject, all by making a simple request.

There are positive aspects regarding the growth and usage of AI, or so I have been told. If you are, for instance, one of the many people who has trouble expressing yourself or making a speech or doing research, AI should be able to help with those things. If it works as it is designed, artificial intelligence should actually improve peoples' lives, as it should ease issues involving communication and learning. Everyone should have the opportunity to be able to reap the benefits of such technology.

People being people, however, it is inevitable that this technology will be used in ways detrimental to society or in ways sillier than can one can imagine. But now, of course, I am more frightened than ever. If AI develops a sense of humor, such as that shown in this story, we are definitely doomed.

Printed in Great Britain
by Amazon

37914063R00025